CW00473928

– About the Author

Ramsey had always been fascinated by the voices of the past. In parchments and scrolls, kings and warriors shouted their tales, while others whispered. However, for Ramsey, the true intrigue lay in the unsung voices, those marginalized and often rendered invisible by the very language historians used to describe them.

"Dialogues Through Time: Pronouns and the Voices of History" began as a pet project. An exploration into how pronouns shaped, and often limited, our understanding of historical narratives. How did the choice of 'he' or 'she', 'they' or 'it', shape our perception of events, of importance, of relevance?

Exploring Identity through Conjectural Conversations

This book utilizes imaginative dialogue between iconic historical figures to simulate insightful debate on the complex modern issue of gender pronouns. While fictional, the conversations reflect extensive research into the lives and perspectives of the featured individuals. The author artfully conjures how these influential voices may have opined on this contemporary topic using their distinct dialects and extrapolated mindsets. The historical contexts and viewpoints are simulated to intellectually reflect the times, though the specific views on pronouns cannot be definitively known. This unique format brings history to life, using informed imagination to simulate spirited discourse spanning centuries regarding an increasingly relevant issue. The debates illuminate multifaceted stances, challenging readers' assumptions with these hypothetical simulations of famous minds grappling with shifting norms. Though conjectural, the dialogues offer an absorbing prism through which to examine the evolution of gender identity from vaunted icons rendered more accessible.

The Power of Pronouns:

The pronouns had taken root in the language of the people, enabling them to express their gender identity with greater ease and accuracy than ever before. They spread like a virus, replacing the traditionally accepted forms of address with something new, something that was more inclusive, less binary.

However, while the pronouns opened up new possibilities for self-expression, they also came with a set of expectations and standards that were difficult to live up to – a strict set of rules and guidelines that dictated how one's gender was to be expressed, as well as what was and wasn't acceptable. This caused confusion and anxiety among many individuals, who suddenly found themselves adhering to a new standard of identity that was both liberating and restrictive.

Ultimately, the adoption of pronouns was a necessary step in the evolution of language and identity. As time went on, people grew more comfortable using them and eventually, these pronouns became a normal part of everyday life. In the end, their presence allowed individuals to express themselves in ways that would have previously been impossible.

Language has always been an essential part of how people express their gender identity, and the introduction of gender-neutral pronouns has revolutionized this process. But, as with any new development, there are also potential pitfalls that can arise depending on how they are used. While these pronouns have opened up new possibilities for self-expression—especially for those who identify as nonbinary or genderqueer—they can also create a false sense of inclusion if not used correctly.

In order to ensure meaningful inclusion, it is important to recognize that gender is more than just pronouns. An individual's full expression includes much more than words; it encompasses clothing and hairstyle choices, actions and behavior, physical features—all of which play into our perception of someone's gender. Therefore, greater attention must be paid to the full spectrum of gender expression in order to foster true acceptance and understanding among all individuals.

The use of pronouns should be just one element in a greater effort towards inclusivity—not the sole focus. By properly recognizing and respecting every aspect of an individual's identity, we can create a society that recognizes everyone as valid and worthy—regardless of their pronouns.

Furthermore, the onus to understand and respect an individual's pronoun choice is placed upon the listener or the reader, overburdening them in communication exchange. Therefore, while this inclusive tactic is useful to some individuals, it le

The adoption of gender-neutral pronouns has been a major milestone in the evolution of language and identity. However, as with any new development, there are also potential pitfalls that can arise depending on how it is used. While these pronouns provide individuals with another way to express themselves and their gender identity, they can also lead to confusion if not used correctly.

At its core, language is a tool for communication, and when pronouns are used outside of their original context—e.g., an individual using a pronoun that does not match their gender identity—it can lead to misunderstandings and miscommunication. This is especially true when communicating with those who are unfamiliar with the concept of gender-neutral pronouns. Additionally, given the complexities of gender expression, it is important to recognize that pronouns alone do not accurately reflect someone's full identity; rather, they should be seen as just one element in a larger spectrum of gender expression.

Ultimately, while the use of diverse pronouns has opened up new possibilities for self-expression, it is important to remember that language must remain first and foremost a medium for effective communication. In order for society to truly embrace acceptance and understanding of all individuals—regardless of their pronouns—we must take into account both verbal and nonverbal aspects of language use in order to foster meaningful inclusion.

The introduction of gender-neutral pronouns has been a major milestone in the evolution of language and identity. It has provided individuals with another way to express themselves and their gender identity while also striving for greater inclusivity. However, it is important to recognize the potential pitfalls that can arise when using these pronouns, as their use outside of their original context can lead to confusion and miscommunication.

At its core, language is a tool for communication, and its efficacy relies on its precision and universality. By introducing a multitude of pronouns into everyday conversation, we are subjectifying our language which can lead to misunderstandings between individuals. Furthermore, given the complexities of gender expression, it is important to remember that pronouns alone do not accurately reflect someone's full identity; rather, they should be seen as just one element in a larger spectrum of gender expression.

Ultimately, while the use of diverse pronouns has opened up new possibilities for self-expression, we must take into account both verbal and nonverbal aspects of language use in order to foster meaningful inclusion. In order for society to truly embrace acceptance and understanding of all individuals—regardless of their pronouns—we must strive towards a more universal understanding that goes beyond the mere usage of words.

However, this huge array of pronouns and subjective self-identifications that are detached from common linguistic references can lead to a loss in communication efficiency, with possible misunderstandings arising not from an intolerance but simply from a lack of shared linguistic understandings. Therefore, the rapid, unbounded increase of pronouns may risk eroding the foundational tenets of effective communication. For instance, if we do not agree on what words mean, it is impossible for us to truly communicate.

Contents

Chapter 1

Debating "Pronouns Vs Gender Identity with Martin Luther King Jr

Should we use pronouns to identify each other.

Matin Luther King Jr

In the great, harmonious symphony of human existence, it is evident that we each play a unique, irreplaceable part. Our individual identities, indeed, are our own personal songs-- striking chords of selfness that reverberate within our spirit. Yet, to lean on pronouns as markers of identity may risk reducing the profound, multi-dimensional symphony into a simplistic scale. While extraordinary advancements of understanding have unearthed the complexity of gender identity, it's important to remember that none of us is defined solely by our gender. We are a compilation of our passions, our pursuits, our relationships, and our experiences. In my vision of a real dream world, we'd strive to know one another on a deeper level than mere pronouns can encapsulate. The essence of our spirits past the gender construct, to the heart and soul of the individual. In that world, we do not see each other as generic labels, but as the intricate, expansive melodies we are.

Opposition

While it commendable to seek understanding beyond mere outward identifiers, it is important to acknowledge that pronouns play a significant role in expressing one's gender identity and validating their sense of self. Although we are complex beings with identities that extend beyond gender, gender remains an integral part of how we perceive ourselves and others. Just as we use names to affirm our individuality, pronouns serve to affirm our gender identities. For many, particularly those who identify as transgender or non-binary, using the correct pronouns can be incredibly affirming and an important recognition of their identity. It does not reduce our complex identity to a single dimension, but rather acknowledges and respects an important part of who we are. This isn't about labels, but about validating and acknowledging that part of someone's identity.

Matin Luther King Jr

While it is without question that our gender identity forms an integral part of our experience, we must be cautious not to mistake acknowledgement for confinement. Certainly, using personal pronouns that align with an individual's gender identity can serve as a sign of respect. However, the risk stands that the over-emphasis on the importance of pronouns may inadvertently put forth a narrative that confines individuals to the box of their gender identity, overshadowing the vast ocean of their individuality. Such may unintentionally perpetuate the very societal norms about gender that we aim to dismantle. True freedom and equality lie not in the segregation of gender identities, but in the unification of our common experiences as human beings. The strength of our society is not reflected by the accuracy of the pronouns we use, but by the depth of understanding and mutual respect we have for one another.

Opposition

The emphasis on pronouns does not confine, rather it liberates individuals by allowing them to express their gender identity authentically. This does not undermine the richness of their individuality, but rather supports it. Societal norms about gender are not dismantled by ignoring these aspects of identity, but by acknowledging and respecting them. Clumping everyone together does not promote unity, it erases the diverse experiences and identities within our society. Using correct pronouns is not about societal strength, it is about individual respect. It's giving people the autonomy to define themselves and recognizing their right to do so. Everyone is entitled to their own identity and everyone else has a social responsibility to respect that.

Matin Luther King Jr

I appreciate the sentiments you've shared, regarding the value of individual agency and respect for one's chosen identity. However, I maintain the potential for a beautiful paradox to emerge whereby the emphasis on pronouns could potentially hinder the very liberation we seek to achieve. With a panoptic focus on gender identity alone, an individual's multifaceted dimensions may inadvertently be overlooked, their experiences assumed or stereotyped based purely on gendered assumptions. It is the richness of our shared experiences in all their diverse variety, not the compartmentalization of our identities, that fuels genuine understanding and respect for one another. I aspire for a world filled not only with the mutual respect of each other's identities, but also the recognition of our shared experiences beyond the confinement of gender, race, or creed.

Chapter 2

Debating Pronouns & Gender Identity Debate with Joe Biden

Should we use pronouns to identify each other

Joe Biden

Pronouns are more than mere labels, they're a vital part of our identity, reflecting who we are to ourselves and the world. They stand as symbols of self-expression and individuality, mirroring our rational capacity to self-identify. This extends beyond binary masculine and feminine tags: gender identity isn't black or white, it's a spectrum. Just as we don't question the necessity of pronouns for men and women, we shouldn't challenge their use for those who identify outside this binary. The use of correct pronouns acknowledges the complexity of human identity, fostering inclusivity, dialogue, and mutual respect. After all, what simpler way is there to respect someone's self-identification than to address them as they prefer?

Opposition

While it is true that pronouns can be integral for self-expression and identity, it is worth considering the practical implications of elevating them to such a high status. Language is a tool meant to facilitate communication, not to cause confusion. In this context, the introduction of a seemingly infinite spectrum of gender pronouns might lead to miscommunication, misunderstandings, or even unintentional offense. Furthermore, complementing the traditional binary system with a spectrum can place an excessive burden on individuals to constantly remember or predict others' preferred pronouns. Lastly, focusing too much on gender identity could shift attention away from the more pressing issues that LGBTQ+ individuals face, such as discrimination and violence.

Joe Biden

While it's true that language serves as a tool for communication, it's also a reflection of societal progress and inclusivity. As our understanding of gender identity evolves, so too must our language. The introduction of personalized pronouns doesn't pave the way for misunderstanding or offense, but rather acts as a bridge towards empathy and acceptance. We will make mistakes, but these are opportunities for education and growth. The 'burden' of remembering one's pronouns is insignificant in comparison to the affirmation it provides someone about their identity. As for diverting attention, recognizing and respecting gender identity doesn't undermine the fight against discrimination and violence. Oppositely, it underpins it: acknowledging individuals' chosen pronouns can help dismantle harmful stereotypes, thus contributing to an environment where every person is valued for who they are, not who society dictates they should be.

Opposition

While the quest for inclusivity is an admirable one, the explosion of personalized pronouns does not necessarily signify progress, but rather fragmentation. Language, as a social tool, operates based on mutual understanding. It cannot serve its primary function if it does not foster clear, effective communication. The current system of he/she/they pronouns is already diverse and inclusive, being able to cover identities across the spectrum without causing significant disruption or confusion. A move towards stringently personalized pronouns can lead to an inadvertent obsession with labels, instead of focusing on the person beyond the tag. This can feed into the societal habit of boxing people into categories, a trend that we are trying to move away from. Additionally, societal focus should shift more towards acceptance and less on 'correct' linguistic usage. The barometer for acceptance shouldn't rest on whether one remembers an individual's specific pronouns, but rather, on their behavior and attitudes towards that individual.

Joe Biden

While our aim should always be focusing on the person rather than the labels, using appropriate pronouns is a part of acknowledging and validating an individual's identity. It's not about fragmenting society or overwhelming language, it's about creating a more inclusive conversation that specifically recognizes each person's unique sense of self. The notion that the existing pronoun framework is sufficient because it is 'already diverse and inclusive' is antithetical to the very spirit of progress. As our understanding of gender identity evolves, so too should our language. This doesn't lead to an obsession with labels but allows us to move beyond boxing people into broad categories, and instead, affirming their chosen identity. Indeed, acceptance goes beyond mere linguistic usage, but language is an intrinsic part of how we express acceptance. Respecting someone's chosen pronouns, far from being a burdensome societal expectation, is an integral expression of that respect. Yes

Chapter 3

Debating 'Pronouns vs Gender Identity with Donald Trump

Should we use pronouns to identify each other

Donald Trump

Listen folks, people have the right to be recognized for who they truly are, okay? It's about respect, it's about liberty. Our forefathers didn't throw tea into a harbor for nothing, right? When an individual chooses their pronouns, it's an assertion of their identity, and we should respect that, big league. It's a free country, people should have the freedom to express themselves however they see fit. Period. Not recognizing an individual's chosen pronouns, it's like saying, "Hey, I don't respect your individual liberty," and that's not what America's about. Believe me folks, it's a matter of basic respect and freedom.

Opposition

A society based on mutual respect and acceptance can only evolve when we acknowledge each other's chosen identities. Using the correct pronouns is not only about personal freedom and liberty, it's also about fostering understanding and empathy among individuals. For people who identify outside the traditional binary genders, pronouns like "they," "them," or "theirs" convey a sense of belonging and validate their identity in broad social terms. By using their chosen pronouns, we're acknowledging their identity, promoting inclusivity, and minimizing the psychological distress often experienced by these individuals. The crux of the issue is not just about individual liberty, but collective acceptance and respect.

Donald Trump

Look, we have a country that is based on liberties and the recognition of individual identities and respect. But let me tell you this right now – there's an irony in limiting pronouns to just "he" or "she." It's restrictive, folks, really restrictive, and that is not, believe me, what our freedom is about. Insisting on using only traditional pronouns actually runs contrary to such values of freedom, liberty, and individual rights that we hold dearly. Have you heard of non-binary people, those who don't identify as merely male or female? It's always been there. We must be inclusive, it's not just a me, you, him or her country – it is an everyone country. Allowing people to identify with the pronouns that truly reflect them, it nurtures understanding, it promotes acceptance – it's about making America, our America, great for everyone.

Opposition

Inclusion and respect for individuals' identities certainly form the bedrock of a compassionate society. Nevertheless, granting people the freedom to choose their pronouns isn't simply about reducing restrictions; it's about creating a society that acknowledges and celebrates diversity. Expanding the range of pronouns beyond the gender binary is an essential step toward fostering understanding and empathy in society, not just for those who are non-binary, but for everyone. Understanding that people's identities go beyond the traditional "he" or "she" pronouns will encourage discussions about gender identity and expression, fostering a society that's more aware and accepting of the complex nature of human identity. Therefore, promoting the use of diversified pronouns not only satisfies the principles of freedom and individual rights but also contributes to an empathetic and understanding society.

Donald Trump

I'm glad you mentioned diversity, its truly fantastic, isn't it? The fact of the matter is that diversity isn't just about acknowledging different skin colors or cultures, it's about accepting different identities. Absolutely! It's about getting with the times, you know? People are unique, people are different. We're not cookie cutters, and that's a beautiful thing, believe me. It's not just about fostering understanding and empathy, it's about living it. When we use diverse pronouns, we're saying, "Hey, I see you, and I respect who you are." That's America, in all its glory. It's incredibly important -- not just for us, but for future generations. So, let's not shy away from diversity -- let's embrace it, big league!

Chapter 4

Debating Pronouns and Gender Identification with Susan B. Anthony

Should we use pronouns to identify each other

Susan B Anthony

In reflecting upon the path of equality and liberty, it is essential to realize that the imposition of gender-specific pronouns can, in many instances, obscure the essence of an individual's identity. To demand that we use pronouns as strict delineators of gender upholds a binary which oftentimes suffocates the expression of varied and valid identities. It chains individuals to societal expectations based on an assigned gender, shunning those who exist beyond the archaic binary. Just as we have fought for women's rights to participate in all socio-political spheres, without being restrained by their gender, the same principles should extend to breaking the limitations imposed by gendered pronouns. By letting individuals choose their pronouns, if they so wish, we are recognizing their right to self-identification and fostering a society that promotes freedom and respect.

Opposition

Freedom and individuality in self-identification hold much merit. However, the complete disregard of gender-specific pronouns may lead to unforeseen complications socially and in communication. Language, along with its components such as pronouns, has evolved to assist in identifying and categorizing, making it easier for one to maneuver in society. In eliminating gendered pronouns, we risk introducing ambiguity and confusion. Furthermore, it isn't necessary to entirely dispose of gendered pronouns to respect an individual's identity. Pronouns can co-exist alongside the recognition of non-binary and transgender identities. As society evolves, so do languages and their norms. The inclusion of gender-neutral pronouns such as 'they' or 'ze' beautifully exemplifies this evolution. It offers a solution that caters to the need for self-expression without negating the necessity and simplicity offered by traditional gender-specific pronouns.

Susan B Anthony

While recognizing the concern around potential ambiguity in communication, it is pertinent to remember that language is a living, breathing entity that evolves and adapts with society. The existing structure of pronouns and the restrictive association it has with gender roles isn't a consequence of natural evolution as much as it is the enforcement of a binary framework that leaves no space for diversity. As societal understanding of gender identity evolves to be more complex and inclusive, our language should keep pace. If the abolition of slavery, winning of women's rights, and the Civil rights movement have taught us anything, it is that societal norms that seem immutable can be, and should be, challenged when they become an impediment to individual liberty and equality. The possibility of temporary confusion in language is not a justifiable reason to deny individuals their rightful freedom to self-identify and evade the limiting boundaries of binary gender norms.

Opposition

Yes, the society and its norms change, but chaos can't be the method of change. Radical change, such as the complete eradication of gender-specific pronouns, can result in confusion. Learning, implementing, and most importantly, accepting this big shift would be challenging for the vast majority of people. It reduces the affordability of change, especially for non-English speaking communities and older generations. Furthermore, discarding gendered pronouns doesn't mean discarding the biases associated with genders altogether. Issues such as inequality, discrimination, and stereotyping exist beyond the sphere of language. They must be addressed directly through societal and legislative changes. The inclusion and recognition of a broader range of pronouns, however, are more realistic and less risky alternatives. They facilitate an environment for everyone to be comfortable with their identities, while keeping the functionality of the language intact.

Susan B Anthony

The assertion that incorporating personal pronouns might result in chaos or confusion does not consider the capacity for human learning and adaptation. Throughout history, humans have adjusted to diverse language features, dialects, and lingual evolutions, so the inclusion of diverse pronouns seems as a natural flow of linguistic adaptation. Moreover, the use of gendered pronouns isn't merely a linguistic issue; it is linked inextricably to societal perceptions and biases. While it is true that eliminating gendered pronouns won't necessarily end biases, it is a step towards recognizing and validating individual identities. Adapting language, which is a tool we use every day, sends a powerful message of acceptance and acknowledgement. Lastly, suggesting the continuation of gendered pronouns overlooks the contention that this binary has often been oppressive and limiting. Including more pronouns and creating space for self-identification is not radical but a much-needed progressive change.

Opposition

While human capacity for learning and adapting is undeniable, we need to also consider the diversity and disparity in access to education, socio-economic conditions and cultural nuances globally. Transition away from gender pronouns requires considerable educational resources which not every region is privileged to invest in. A more inclusive linguistic system, on the other hand, would be gradual and more accommodating of these disparities. Furthermore, language evolution is more effective when it occurs organically responding to societal changes, rather than by forcible imposition. Lastly, it's worth noting that identities are multidimensional. The association of one's gender with their identity is as limiting or as liberating as one perceives it to be. Respect for one's chosen identity, regardless of whether it aligns with conventional binaries or not, is of paramount importance. It starts with accepting and respecting the use of preferred pronouns, within the existing system of gendered pronouns.

Susan B Anthony

It is undeniable that educational resources are not equally accessible around the world, and that language evolution occurs most effectively when it arises naturally. However, arguing for the continuation of using gendered pronouns while respecting a small set of new ones might not alleviate the discomfort that non-binary or transgender individuals often feel. The presence of gendered pronouns itself underlines a binary that is more oppressive to some than liberating, reinforcing a societal division that we are striving to overcome. The existence of gender-neutral pronouns in some languages is evidence that societies can thrive without the enforced gender binary in their language. Therefore, while maintaining sensitivity towards the pace of change and people's ability to adapt, we should visualize and strive for an equitable linguistic system that does not bind individuals to a gender binary.

Chapter 5

Debating Pronoun Introduction: Necessary or Not? with Mary Wollstonecraft

Should we introduce pronouns to identify each other Gender

Mary Wollstonecraft

Your argument that education and familiarization can cure all miscommunication may not be accurate in all scenarios. Not all societies have the resources, time, or inclination to invest in such changes. The change in language, particularly the introduction of new pronouns, might be too swift or complex for some. Language, by nature, is an organic, spontaneous construct; enforcing change might undermine its organic essence. Moreover, respect and dignity should be universal values, transcending the bounds of language or any other kind of identification. The fear is that a focus on pronouns might divert attention from these values, promoting a culture where the use of correct pronouns might wrongly be seen as the only marker of respect. It is paramount that we recognize that the essence of respect and dignity lies not in the correct use of pronouns, but in treating each other as equal rational beings.

Opposition

The virtue of humanity ought to shine through one's actions, regardless of the gender one identifies with; indeed, the fundamental principles of justice do not require such a prescriptive delineation. Putting such emphasis on pronouns prioritizes identity over actions and overlooks the commonality of human reason. The challenge, therefore, is not in introducing pronouns but rather in educating society to respect individual autonomy and acknowledge each person's capacity to reason, irrespective of what pronoun they may use. The complication of multiple new pronouns could potentially lead to unnecessary confusion and the risk of negative social and cultural impacts. We must prioritize respect for human reasoning and individual autonomy, and not distract from this by overemphasizing identification pronouns.

Mary Wollstonecraft

While I do agree with the importance of human reason and individual autonomy, I argue that the introduction of pronouns can support this rather than detract from it. In a society that is complex and diverse, recognizing a person's choice of pronouns does not devalue their actions, but pays respect to their autonomy. It allows individuals to portray their identity accurately and by literally being addressed by the right pronouns in their interactions, people often feel respected and acknowledged. The complexity of new pronouns can be mitigated through education and awareness raising, thus fostering a more inclusive and tolerant society. In this way, it is not a hindrance but a development in the evolution of language and society.

Opposition

While it cannot be denied that an individual's identity has the right to be acknowledged, we must be wary of the tendency to fragment our society into myriad identities, thereby weakening the ties that bind us as human beings. A preoccupation with pronouns and personal identity can lead to a self-absorbed society where individual preferences take precedence over common unity. Additionally, language, as a tool for communication, should maintain a degree of simplicity and universal comprehensibility. Introduction of a plethora of pronouns might complicate discourse and diminish comprehensibility. Furthermore, respectful treatment of individuals should not hinge solely on using correct pronouns; instead, it should be deeply rooted in the perception of each individual as an autonomous, rational being deserving dignity and respect by virtue of their humanity.

Mary Wollstonecraft

While your concerns about societal fragmentation and language complexity are valid, I believe they underestimate the flexibility and adaptability of both society and language. Society has always been diverse, and recognizing this through use of chosen pronouns doesn't fragment us, but rather reflects our reality. It actually fosters a more inclusive environment where everyone feels seen and respected. As for language, it has continuously evolved through history, adapting to different needs and contexts. It's worth noting that a complex language can also be an inclusive and respectful one. Pronouns, like any other aspect of language, can be learned and normalized through use. Using correct pronouns doesn't replace the need for respect, it demonstrates it.

Opposition

Change, while often necessary, must be approached with due diligence, particularly when it involves manipulating our linguistic conventions. While society has indeed been characterized by diversity and change, language's primary role as a tool for effective communication must not be compromised. Imposing a diverse and complex range of pronouns could lead to significant communicative confusion and misunderstanding. Furthermore, an overemphasis on individual identity can tip the scale towards a level of radical individualism that could potentially erode our collective societal values. By putting undue importance on our personal identities and preferences, we risk diminishing our understanding of our shared humanity, leading to societal fragmentation. It is crucial, therefore, to strike a balance that respects individual identity while preserving the principle of universal human rights and dignity that bind us as a society.

Mary Wollstonecraft

Although it's understood that an abrupt change in language can create misunderstanding, we shouldn't underestimate the capacity of society to learn and adapt. History is rich with examples of significant linguistic shifts that have been absorbed and normalized over time. Introducing new pronouns doesn't impose a threat to communication, but evolves it to reflect the reality of diverse gender identities. Concerning the worry of promoting radical individualism, it's important to differentiate between individualism that isolates and individualism that fosters inclusivity. Acknowledging someone's pronouns doesn't erode our collective societal values. On the contrary, it strengthens the essence of those values by creating an environment where everyone's identity is respected. The ultimate goal is a society where using the right pronouns is as normal as using someone's name, thus reinforcing our shared humanity and collective respect for individual rights and dignity.

Opposition

While it is indeed true that society has the capacity to learn and adapt to changes in language, it is also crucial to note that this adaptation should not result in unnecessary strain or tension among its members. The process of incorporating an expansive range of pronouns into everyday lexicon may inadvertently impose burdens on those struggling to grasp the shift, especially among older generations. It could also lead to inadvertent harm, as unintentional misgendering due to unfamiliarity with new pronouns may further damage societal cohesion. Additionally, while individualism that fosters inclusivity is indeed desirable, it shouldn't promote emphasis on identity props at the expense of the core values of respect and dignity for all. The virtue of respect shouldn't lie in the correct use of pronouns, but rather in recognition of our individual moral and rational capacities.

Mary Wollstonecraft

While recognizing the apprehensions of introducing multiple pronouns including challenges faced by older generations, we must not discount the continuous learning and evolution that defines our societal growth. Societal norms are a testament to changes embraced over time and new linguistic appropriations should not be an exception. The misgendering concerns you raise are precisely why we need to normalize and educate people about pronoun use, to eliminate accidental disrespect and ensure everyone's identity is acknowledged. Respect for moral and rational capacities is not mutually exclusive with respect for one's pronouns - they complement each other in fostering overall individual respect. Education and familiarization are key to mastering this change, not avoidance due to potential temporary uncertainties.

Chapter 6

Debating Pronouns: A Fundamental Tool for Acknowledgement with Benjamin Franklin

Should we use pronouns to identify each other

While pronouns can serve a practical purpose in language, we should not place excessive importance on them as a fundamental tool for acknowledgement. Pronouns often create unnecessary divisions among individuals, leading to an emphasis on identity politics rather than fostering genuine understanding and connection. By fixating on pronouns, we risk alienating people who may not conform to traditional gender categories, imposing limitations on their self-expression and individuality. Instead, we should focus on acknowledging and respecting one another based on character, values, and actions, rather than reducing individuals to mere pronouns.

Opposition

It is important to recognize that pronouns serve a crucial role in acknowledging and affirming individuals' identities. By using the correct pronouns, we show respect and validation for how individuals choose to identify themselves. Pronouns are not simply a matter of convenience or political correctness; they are an essential aspect of affirming someone's gender identity and acknowledging their existence. Ignoring or disregarding pronouns can lead to feelings of invisibility, erasure, and even discrimination. By embracing and using pronouns, we create a more inclusive society where everyone feels seen and valued.

Benjamin Franklin

While it is important to respect and acknowledge individuals, placing such a heavy emphasis on pronouns as a fundamental tool for acknowledgement can lead to a narrowing of perspectives and stifling of meaningful discourse. Language is a dynamic and evolving system, and pronouns are just one aspect of it. By fixating on pronouns, we risk reducing conversations to a focus on identity labels rather than engaging in substantive discussions about ideas, values, and experiences. True acknowledgement lies in our ability to listen, understand, and empathize with others, rather than solely relying on pronouns as a measure of respect.

Opposition

While pronouns may not be the sole measure of acknowledgement, they play a crucial role in affirming individuals' identities and fostering an inclusive environment. By using the correct pronouns, we demonstrate a level of understanding and respect for someone's self-identification. Pronouns are not just identity labels; they are a means of validating and affirming someone's lived experience. Dismissing the importance of pronouns can contribute to marginalization and exclusion. Embracing pronouns as a tool for acknowledgement allows us to create a more inclusive society where individuals feel seen, heard, and valued.

Benjamin Franklin

While pronouns can play a role in acknowledging individuals, the significance placed on them is disproportionate. We should prioritize understanding and connecting with others based on their character and actions, rather than fixating on pronouns. Elevating pronouns to a fundamental tool for acknowledgement may inadvertently create divisions and hinder genuine communication. By focusing on broader aspects of identity and common values, we can foster a more inclusive and understanding society.

Chapter 7

Debating Pronoun Identification with Bill Clinton

Should we use pronouns to identify each other

Bill Clinton

Well, I do respect your viewpoint, but allow me to offer a different perspective. My belief is that while pronouns can certainly serve as a way to identify each other, they might not be the most appropriate or sufficient way to do so. The English language, like many others, has traditionally operated upon a binary system of gender identification— he or she, him or her. But as society is becoming more cognizant and accepting of those who do not identify strictly within this binary, it raises a concern. Relying heavily on pronouns could inadvertently marginalize those who identify outside of the gender binary or those who prefer not to be identified by their gender at all. In essence, while pronouns could be a quick way to refer to someone, their use should be supplemented, or sometimes substituted, with other identifiers that more fully respect and acknowledge the complexities of individual identity.

Opposition

You argue against identifying each other using pronouns, citing potential marginalization of those who identify outside of the gender binary. You suggest using other identifiers that more fully represent individual identity, which is undeniably valid. However, advocating for the complete disregarding of pronouns in identification might pose expected challenges. Pronouns fulfill an important function in communication, they provide efficiency and coherence. If we were to completely replace them with 'individual identifiers,' conversations could become confusing and inefficient, making daily communication challenging. Instead, perhaps the solution is to adapt and expand our use of pronouns to be more inclusive. After all, language is a tool, and like all tools, it can be modified to better fit the needs of the people using it. As this is a current social issue, the consciousness about the fluidity and non-binary nature of gender is increasing. More inclusive pronouns are coming into use, including "they/them/their" utilized in a singular manner, and neopronouns such as ze/hir. So, rather than eliminating our use of pronouns for identification, perhaps the emphasis should instead be on broadening or modifying our existing linguistic structures to better accommodate evolving understandings of identity.

Bill Clinton

Indeed, one cannot deny the role of efficiency and coherence in language use and communication. However, the issue that lies at hand is not about completely eliminating pronouns. The argument for using other identifiers besides pronouns is about promoting diversity, inclusivity, and respect towards individuals and their chosen identities. Our language, undeniably, should and does evolve to accommodate the changes in our society, and it's important to note that modifications such as the inclusion of non-binary pronouns are already steps in this direction. However, without diminishing the role of pronouns, it's beneficial to reframe our understanding and usage of identifiers. Just like when we converse, we incorporate names, titles, or roles along with pronouns, we can be more mindful to embrace identifiers which people associate themselves with. This approach not only enriches our language but also fosters an environment where individuals feel acknowledged and validated.

Opposition

Your assertion about incorporating diverse identifiers in conversation is commendable, yet it encounters a predicament central to real-world applicability: Can such practice ensure smooth, uninterrupted communication, especially in quick exchanges? Keep in mind the cognitive load that could potentially arise when one is tasked to continually switch between different identifying terms that an individual prefers. To a certain extent, this might impede efficient communication. I argue that, instead, we should strive to build a balance, a linguistic ecosystem where pronouns and other identifiers co-exist. Pronouns provide efficiency, and as you rightly pointed out, language continues to evolve to be more inclusive. At the same time, we must make an effort to use other identifiers respected by individuals. The solution lies in a balanced utilization rather than heavily leaning towards one and forgoing the other. Meanwhile, promoting education and sensitization about respectful language use should be prioritized to build a more accepting society.

Bill Clinton

I do agree that balance plays a key role in our discussion. However, it's also critical to recognize that the notion of balance you're proposing presumes that the benefits and challenges of pronouns and other identifiers are relative and the same for everybody. The reality is not as homogenous. Different individuals have divergent experiences and preferences when it comes to identification, making it impossible to impose a single language usage standard that everyone finds comfortable and respectful. For some, the ease of communication offered by utilizing pronouns is paramount, while for others, the affirmation in identity delivered through other identifiers is crucial. Ultimately, the "balance" is subjective and should be defined by the individuals involved, which goes back to the importance of recognizing and respecting other identifiers along with pronouns. Considering this, continuous education, awareness and sensitivity towards individual preferences become imperative in fostering inclusive interactions.

Chapter 8

Debating Pronoun Identification: Yay or Nay with Abraham Lincoln

Should we use pronouns to identify each other

Abraham Lincoln

My esteemed interlocutor, I place before you the proposition that the proposed need for pronoun identification lifts a burden that should not have to be borne by every individual. In a society founded on the inalienable rights of freedom and personal integrity, it is not becoming of us to subject each person to the necessity of announcing what should be by all accounts private information about how they perceive themselves. Implicit within this are underlying issues of personal integrity and the freedom of the individual to define and redefine their identity on their own terms and timeframe. If we were to consider the necessity of announcing one's pronouns casually in every conversation, it is clear we may be forcing intrusive conversations about deeply personal aspects of a person's identity whether they wish to have such discussions or not. Therefore, it stands to reason that the obstacle to understanding and acceptance cannot be solved through obligatory linguistic changes, but through fostering a more tolerant and open-minded society.

Opposition

While it is true that each individual should have the right to self-definition and maintaining the confidentiality of their private information, the idea of pronoun identification also serves as a platform for visibility and acceptance of diverse gender identities. It is not just about obligatory linguistic changes, but it is also about acknowledging and validating the identity of each person. When individuals express their preferred pronouns, they are not just stating information about themselves, but they are communicating how they wish to be respected. By using correct pronouns, one acknowledges the individuality and importance of a person's chosen identity. Therefore, pronoun identification can be seen not an invasion of privacy, but an expansion of the minimum standard for treating each other with respect and dignity.

Abraham Lincoln

My honored opponent, your notion of respect and dignity is indeed valid, yet it seems to place a considerable and unbalanced onus upon the speaker. If we espouse that people must invariably rethink their language to accommodate a broad spectrum of identities, we risk creating an apprehension toward discourse, stifling conversation and diminishing the natural flow of human communication. Although respect and dignity are of the utmost importance, it is worth considering whether such a rigid requirement might lead to a form of speech that, while inclusive, may also feel overly prescriptive and removed from the authentic expression of our identities and emotions. While we endeavor to embrace diversity, we must also ensure that conversations remain sincere and approachable. As such, might we not better serve respect and dignity by advocating a shared understanding that sometimes, people will use the wrong pronouns, and that each of us bears a responsibility for graciously correcting and learning, rather than the current proposal which could lead to a fear of engagement?

Opposition

Although the potential for conversation to become rigid or hard is a genuine concern, it is important to note that language evolves over time, adjusting to the societal changes and needs. Pronoun identification wouldn't stifle conversation, instead, it would enrich it, making it more inclusive and representative of all identities. It's a way to bring forth the unaddressed identities into the normative discourse. While mistakes would undoubtedly occur, they shouldn't be feared but seen as opportunities for further understanding and fostering inclusiveness. The implementation of pronoun identification wouldn't endanger the authenticity of our expression instead, it broadens our understanding of identities. Moreover, the apprehension towards addressing numerous identities would also decrease over time as these pronouns get integrated into everyday language, eventually becoming the norm rather than the exception.

Abraham Lincoln

My honorable opponent, your viewpoint is acknowledged and appreciated. However, it is prudent to note that while language indeed evolves, the speed and nature of its evolution ought to be organic and not forced. It is a fact universally acknowledged that language is a reflection of a society's culture. Mandating the use of pronouns, rather than letting such changes arise naturally from societal developments, could infringe upon that natural evolution of language. Furthermore, while the intention of such mandates is to foster inclusiveness, they could potentially be seen as cultivating an environment of hyper-sensitivity, where individuals perceive every misstep in the use of pronouns as an intentional slight or offense. This could conceivably lead to further divisions in society, rather than bridging gaps. It is arguably far better to encourage understanding and education about gender issues and personal pronouns, rather than enforcing compulsory regulations.

Chapter 9

Debating Pronouns for Gender Identification with John F Kennedy

Should we introduce pronouns to identify each other Gender

John F Kennedy

While respecting the importance of individual identities, it is crucial to acknowledge the potential complication that arises with the introduction of multiple pronouns for gender identification. When we focus on implementing varying gender pronouns, I'm afraid we inadvertently divert our attention from issues of greater urgency such as gender equality and elimination of gender-based discrimination. Yes, we ought to respect personal identities, but we need not to lose sight of the bigger cause. We live in an increasingly globalized world, where we interact with individuals from diverse cultural backgrounds whose languages may not have equivalent pronouns, thereby creating a potential barrier to communication. In addition, asking institutions, small businesses and the educational sector to adapt to a rapidly changing landscape of gender pronouns could result in added complexities and resources that could be better utilized to create substantive equality rather than symbolic recognition. Thus, it is essential to concentrate on formulating policies seeking to end discrimination and promoting equality at all levels, rather than focusing on sustainable identity recognition.

Opposition

While it's essential not to divert from paramount issues like gender discrimination and inequality, the usage of correct pronouns for gender identification doesn't detract from these causes but instead, aids in addressing them. By using someone's chosen pronouns, we not only respect and validate their identity, but we also take a step towards dismantling harmful gender stereotypes. This recognition can play a critical role in reducing mental health issues prevalent in people whose identities are not socially accepted or understood. Furthermore, the potential for communication barriers and organizational implementation issues is manageable and should not deter societal progress. We've successfully integrated other profound societal changes in the past where communication and organizational structures were impacted. This progression calls for a collective effort to educate and adapt, which, while requiring some time and understanding, is undoubtedly achievable.

John F Kennedy

The dedication to dismantling harmful gender stereotypes and reducing mental health issues is indeed a justified cause, but allow us to think about the broad perspective of this matter. Change on such a vast, linguistic scale can be slower and more arduous than one acknowledges. Language has deep roots, and its transformation entails efforts beyond just an individual or group's commitment. The complication that may rise due to multiple pronouns can introduce confusion, particularly for those amongst us whose first language is not English or those belonging to older generations. In a world where language variations and accents already pose significant challenges to communication and understanding, the introduction of a more extensive array of gender pronouns may exacerbate these barriers, unintentionally contributing to exclusion, rather than the intended inclusion. Hence, the pursuit of fostering understanding, respect, and acceptance of diversity in gender identities, and mitigating mental health issues prevalent in the population needs to be addressed at a wider scope where implementation of multiple gender pronouns may not adequately fulfill the broader goal.

Opposition

While the concern about potential linguistic confusion is valid, it's vital to remember that language evolves over time, adapting to mirror societal changes. In fact, the English language has absorbed numerous changes in the past, many of which seemed unthinkable during their inception, yet are now fully integrated within daily lexicon. Moreover, the process of gender identification through pronouns is not about forcing a rapid, overnight language transformation, it's about introducing a concept of respect and understanding to a broader audience. Potential initial confusion doesn't invalidate the need for language to reflect society's growing understanding of gender diversity. For individuals navigating the process of gender identification, having their pronouns recognized has significant psychological benefits that shouldn't be disregarded due to temporary communication challenges. Furthermore, as we become increasingly digital, many non-English languages are also developing ways to incorporate gender-neutral terms, showing that this is not just an English-centric matter. Therefore, incorporating appropriate gender pronouns doesn't Stymie the cause but works in tandem with it.

John F Kennedy

Whilst I appreciate the argument that language evolves over time, concurrently, we cannot disregard the fact that such evolution has always unfolded organically, not through imposition. Indeed, lexicon has absorbed changes throughout history, but most of these changes have taken place over extended periods and were not necessarily introduced as policies to be adhered to. The transformation of language to reflect societal change is a natural and gradual process, catalyzed by common societal understandings and not pressure. A coerced change may indeed create opposition and confusing outcomes rather than fostering acceptance and understanding, which is the underlying motive of the initiative. Additionally, the potential confusion and communication barriers hinted at are not necessarily temporary. For many, language is deeply ingrained, and change can be challenging, particularly for those older or those not proficient in the English language. Therefore, the core focus should be on promoting understanding and acceptance on a societal level, and let language evolve naturally, as it has done throughout history.

Chapter 10

Debating Pronouns as Gender Identifiers: Yes or No? with Ruth Bader Ginsburg

Should we introduce pronouns to identify each other Gender

Ruth Bader Ginsburg

Although I understand your perspective, I oppose the idea that pronouns should be used as mandatory markers of gender identity. Language is a powerful device, and it certainly can signify respect, identity, and inclusivity. Nonetheless, enforcing the usage of gender-specific pronouns, especially in diverse societies, may inadvertently marginalize those who do not identify with the binary system of gender pronouns. It risks imposing an unwarranted burden of declaration, where individuals would be compelled to regularly disclose intimate aspects of their personal identities, even in casual conversations. Rather, respect for personhood ought to extend beyond rigid linguistic structures and may be demonstrated in manifold ways beyond terminology. Au contraire to fostering inclusivity, this measure might fortify divisions and inadvertently marginalize those whose identities defy societal norms.

Opposition

While it may appear that our current pronoun usage sufficiently caters to the majority's experiences, doing this excludes a large number of people who do not fit into this binary gender system. By restricting pronouns as gender identifiers, we further alienate certain individuals, particularly those who identify as transgender, nonbinary, or gender non-conforming. This lack of recognition can lead to negative societal and psychological effects, including a lack of self-esteem, increased rates of mental health issues, and intensified discrimination. Additionally, language is an evolving construct and should change to reflect societal nuances. Adopting a more inclusive approach to pronouns fosters respect and understanding, reinforcing the idea that everyone's identity matters.

Ruth Bader Ginsburg

While I understand your argument, in adopting non-traditional pronoun usage, there exists the potential for greater division and misunderstanding. Language, while evolving, possesses a shared understanding among its speakers. By introducing new pronouns or using traditional ones in unfamiliar ways, we may only encourage confusion and discord. In addition, requesting or requiring others to use certain pronouns could infringe upon an individual's freedom of speech, a cornerstone principle of many societies. Instead of changing pronouns, we could focus on fostering a culture of respect and understanding for all individuals, regardless of their gender, promoting openness and acceptance above linguistic reforms.

Opposition

While respecting an individual's freedom of speech is crucial, it's equally important to prioritize the mental health and well-being of individuals who identify outside of the binary spectrum. Societal acceptance plays a significant part in this—pronouns being a key aspect. It's not solely about the change in language, but about the affirmation and recognition of identities that exist beyond the male-female dichotomy. While it's true that language changes may initially generate confusion, education and dialogue play a fundamental role in mitigating it. History shows us that language evolves to accommodate societal changes and shifts in understanding. So, our language should reflect our progressive understanding of gender. Besides, if non-binary people have adapted to a language that doesn't adequately represent them for centuries, surely cisgender people can adjust to a few additional pronouns.

Ruth Bader Ginsburg

While acknowledging the importance of recognition and affirmation of non-binary identities, it is crucial to note that the establishment of non-traditional pronouns as gender identifiers may not be a universally applicable or accepted solution. The spectrum of gender identities is vast and varied, transcending geographical, cultural, and individual boundaries. Therefore, pronouns, particularly in the English lexicon, may not be universal enough to encompass all these identities satisfactorily. To presume that a handful of additional pronouns could accurately represent the vast spectrum of human gender identity globally could inadvertently oversimplify the complexity of this issue. Instead, promoting respect, acceptance, and understanding towards all gender identities without relying heavily on pronoun usage could serve as a more inclusive and universally applicable solution. We must strive for a society in which one's worth is not determined by adherence to particular gender norms.

Chapter 11

Debating Gender Identification: The Pronoun Debate with Ronald Reagan
Should we introduce pronouns to identify each other Gender

Ronald Reagan

While the underlying intentions of gender pronouns are compassionate and progressive, their implementation introduces a host of practical issues and potential conflicts with fundamental freedoms. For instance, mandated use of preferred pronouns may infringe on First Amendment rights here in the US, as it would compel individuals to express a specific viewpoint. Freedom of speech includes the right not to speak. Beyond the legality, the issue also poses a challenge to the communication as language is a crucial aspect of social interaction and adding complexities to everyday speech could lead to misunderstandings and miscommunications. It must be noted that while as a society we should strive for inclusion and understanding, we also must consider the practical realities and potential unintended consequences of our actions.

Opposition

The assertion that using preferred pronouns may infringe on First Amendment rights largely misconstrues the intent behind encouraging their use. The purpose is not to constrain free speech, but rather to promote respect for each other's identities. This level of mindfulness can create a more inclusive environment that respects individual identities. As for the notion that introducing more specific pronouns will complicate communication, language has always evolved to reflect societal needs. For example, the adoption of new words and expressions in our vernacular hasn't continuously led to mass confusion, but rather enriched our ability to communicate. Also, it is important to remember, that challenging dominant norms can be uncomfortable, but ultimately it is harnessed for the sake of evolution. If we don't reassess and adjust our modes of expression as we evolve socio-culturally, language can become a tool of stagnation rather than progress.

Ronald Reagan

Indeed, promoting respect for each other's identities is an admirable cause, yet it's paramount to remember that respect is a voluntary act of empathy and understanding, not something that can be legislated or imposed. It's a two-sided coin: while we never want anyone to feel disrespected or devalued, we also cannot neglect the necessity for free speech and the exploration of thoughts and ideas, even if they may not align with the dominant mode of thinking.

As for language evolution, it's true that language changes over time, but ideally, these changes occur organically, brought by gradual shifts in the society's consciousness and not through imposition. Words adopted from technological advancements or cultural shifts generally add to our repository of expressions, rather than altering the established ones.

Lastly, progress, in societal terms, is subjective. What counts as progress for one group might not be the same for another. It's the robust and open discourse, even about sensitive issues that makes us truly progressive, maintaining a society tolerant of differing ideas. It's crucial that we don't set a precedent where mainstream narratives can dictate the linguistic behavior and limit the freedom of thought of individuals.

Opposition

While it's true that respect is a voluntary act, using appropriate pronouns permeates beyond mere matters of respect. It directly addresses a person's identity, experiences, and realities. By using correct pronouns, we validate a person's identity and affirm their individuality. As per free speech, it doesn't allow us to disregard a person's humanity or identity. It's not about aligning everybody with a dominant mode of thinking; instead, it's to accept and respect human diversity.

On the issue of language evolution, your argument assumes that evolving pronouns are "imposed" changes, which is an overly simplified view. Many people are choosing these pronouns organically, directly from their experiences and identities, and their use is increasingly socially accepted over time. Language is a social construct and thus evolves with shifts in societal consciousness.

Lastly, progress is indeed subjective, but a society's progress can largely be gauged by how we treat our most marginalized members. Incorporating inclusive pronouns is an essential stride towards acknowledging and validating marginalized gender identities. In conclusion, we should view the use of appropriate pronouns as an expansion of our linguistic behavior to emphasize mutual respect, empathy, and understanding.

Ronald Reagan

Enforcing specific use of pronouns assumes that we are all certain about our gender identities. However, it's worth mentioning that this is a deeply personal journey and not everyone has affirmatively settled into their identity. By enforcing pronoun usage, we may inadvertently pressure these individuals into defining their identity, which has can create additional stress. Furthermore, even within the circle advocating for gender identification through pronouns, there isn't a consensus on an appropriate list of pronouns, demonstrating the complexity and subjective nature of this issue.

Moreover, when it comes to respect, it is a crucial foundation of any thriving society, but making it mandatory through law tends to alienate people. Historically, imposing mandates has caused more division in society rather than unity. Therefore, it's essential to handle this matter with sensitivity rather than imposition.

Finally, regarding the argument that changing our language validates marginalized identities, it's important to realize that validation comes from a feeling of being understood and accepted, not merely called by a correct pronoun. As a society aiming for progress, we should focus more on fostering empathy and understanding about diverse gender identities, rather than addressing the issue superficially through language modification.

Chapter 12

Debating Pronouns and Gender Identification with Princess Diane

Should we introduce pronouns to identify each other Gender

Princess Diane

While the idea of introducing pronouns to identify gender seems inclusive on the surface, it may inadvertently limit individuals in expressing the complexity of their identities. Humans are multiplex beings with identities that often intersect across various dimensions including culture, religion, and experiences. Singular pronouns risk reducing people to one aspect of their identity, thereby 'othering' them and potentially breeding stereotypes. It's crucial we respect and understand each other's unique identities without solely relying on pronouns, and instead, foster environments that embrace diversity and promote dialogue.

Opposition

Enforcing the use of certain pronouns can pose a risk of encroaching upon individual liberties and freedom of speech. While it is important to respect people's chosen identities, it is equally crucial that we do not unintentionally impinge upon the right to express oneself freely. Enforced usage of pronouns might lead to inadvertent mistakes, and consequent punitive actions for these mistakes could create a climate of fear and self-censorship, thus inhibiting open dialogue and understanding about issues related to gender and identity. A more holistic approach could involve educating individuals and fostering empathy, rather than mandating the use of specific words.

Princess Diane

While it is important to preserve individual liberties and freedom of speech, it is equally vital to ensure that these are not used as vehicles for harm or discrimination. Proper use of pronouns can validate and affirm gender identities, rather than infringe upon free speech. An unintentional misstep should not provoke fear if societies cultivate a culture of respect and understanding, where mistakes are viewed as opportunities for growth. Freedom of speech must not be weaponized to validate insensitivity, but rather should inspire empathic understanding towards identities outside one's own experience. Education is indeed essential; however, it goes hand in hand with the respectful use of pronouns - not as a replacement.

Opposition

While it's true that using correct pronouns can validate and affirm gender identities, the reality is that language is a constantly evolving aspect of human culture. Linguistic changes cannot be mandated or enforced effectively, but should be allowed to develop naturally within societies. Relying on legislations or amendments to facilitate language changes can lead to resistances and further polarization of viewpoints. A more effective approach towards respecting and understanding complex gender identities may lie in fostering societal attitudes that embrace diversity, encouraging educational initiatives about gender identities, and promoting dialogues for mutual understanding, rather than focusing solely on language conventions.

Princess Diane

While it's accurate to state that language evolves, it is equally true that humans consciously guide much of this evolution. Social shifts often necessitate changes in language. For example, consider terms like 'Ms.', which came into use to address women without highlighting martial status, a step towards gender equality. Mandating the correct use of pronouns isn't about legislation or enforcement; it's about social etiquette evolving to acknowledge and respect all identities. Education and dialogue are certainly crucial, but the importance of daily language conventions, simple as they may seem, should not be discounted as they can significantly foster or hinder mutual understanding and respect.

Opposition

While it's true that language can change and evolve with societal norms, it's crucial to remember that changes should be organic and not enforced. The usage of 'Ms.' as you've mentioned was a natural outcome out of the need for language to be fair and inclusive. It wasn't enforced via regulations or rules. In the case of pronouns, compelling individuals to use specific ones could potentially create resistance and an unnatural discourse, as individuals may feel their freedom of speech is being threatened. It's vital to allow the population to adapt to these changes fairly and naturally over time. This way, they are more likely to respect and follow the new norms willingly.

Princess Diane

Although it is important to consider an organic evolution of language and societal norms, it is practical that we do not ignore the urgent need for inclusivity in our society. One must remember that changes, especially those deeply rooted in social conventions and expectations, take a considerably long time when left to occur naturally. Meanwhile, marginalized groups continue to suffer from non-recognition and misidentification. Intentional steps towards inclusivity, such as the respectful usage of correct pronouns, catalyze the evolutionary process of societal norms and accelerate the journey towards a more accepting society. Moreover, this is not about compelling anyone, but about educating and promoting understanding of the diversity that enriches humanity, just as we do with any other etiquettes or manners that we teach in society.

Chapter 13

Debating Pronouns for Gender Identification with Rosa Parks

Should we introduce pronouns to identify each other Gender

Rosa Parks

While the intention behind introducing pronouns for gender identification is commendable as it seeks to foster inclusivity, this move could also inadvertently lead to an increase in binaries and segregation. History has shown us that any such labeling often results in an undue emphasis on differences rather than commonalities among individuals. Moreover, it may shift our focus from substantive issues such as equality of rights, fair treatment, and focusing more on aspects of identity, leading us down a road where individuality is defined merely by labels. This could, unintentionally, reinforce stereotypes rather than dismantle them.

Opposition

It is important to bring to the fore the matter of simplification and practicality. The use of personalized pronouns can become complex and challenging to manage in day-to-day communication. All languages have evolved organically with set rules for usage and simplicity for global understanding. In fact, many languages do not even possess gender-specific pronouns. The introduction of personalized pronouns, therefore, might lead to unnecessary complications, miscommunications and even resentment or resistance from those who find it difficult to navigate this evolved linguistic landscape.

Rosa Parks

Understanding that linguistic evolution is an integral part of our societal progress, it is equally essential to protect an individual's freedom to self-identify. However, mandating all individuals to conform to a new system may potentially infringe upon the freedom of those individuals who find solace in traditional gender pronouns. Such a push might foster resentment and backlash merely by imposing a change that many might not necessarily agree with or understand, thereby creating a divisive atmosphere instead of the inclusive one intended. It would be significant to foster a climate where everyone is free to express their identity in the terms they find most appropriate, without enforcing a one-size-fits-all solution on everyone.

Opposition

While it's important to respect the gender identity of all individuals, we also need to consider the broad confusion and complexity this introduces to the audience, acquaintance, or a third person who is unaware of the preferred pronouns of the person being referenced. Failing to use the correct pronoun may result in offending people unintentionally. This results in an extra burden and responsibility on ordinary people to remember and use the right pronouns for each individual, creating a convoluted and tricky social navigation system. A more feasible approach could be to work on societal acceptance of people's chosen identities rather than universally altering language structures which have existed for centuries.

Rosa Parks

While I am well aware that enforcing a universal change in language structure imposes a certain burden on those unfamiliar with the new system, I also invite us to look at the situation from a different perspective. It is essential to remember that language evolves according to societal need. As society becomes more aware and accepting of diverse gender identities, our language needs to reflect that. It may initially seem challenging, but it's not impossible

Several historically male-dominated professions now use gender-neutral language, indicating that inclusive language is not unreachable. Rather than resisting this change, isn't our responsibility to evolve and become more inclusive regardless of the difficulties we might face initially? It is important to recognize that we are in the midst of a genuine societal change, and we need to adapt to preserve the rights and identities of all individuals.

Opposition

Whilst it is indeed the case that language must reflect societal changes, it is crucial to remember that these changes must happen organically and at a pace that society can keep up with. Rapid introduction and enforcement of new linguistic norms risk causing pervasive misunderstandings, confusion, and even unintentional offences. Additionally, while transforming language, it is vital to strike a balance between valuing individual preferences and maintaining the functionality and simplicity of communication. The application of individual, preferred gender pronouns across all public platforms might impede effective communication, as well as lead to a disarray in legal, professional, and institutional documentation. As such, fostering inclusivity should not come at the cost of compromising the ease of communication and day-to-day transactions.

Rosa Parks

I agree with your standpoint on striking a balance, but I believe it's essential to consider that every significant societal and language change is initially met with some level of chaos and confusion. Yes, it could potentially result in some complications in terms of communication or documentation. However, can these logistical inconveniences truly outweigh the necessity for social justice and individual dignity? Predicaments like these have been overcome in the past for other social reforms, and I believe with appropriate planning and time, these issues could be addressed adequately. This change may indeed require some adaptation, but the end goal of a more inclusive society makes it a worthwhile endeavor.

Printed in Great Britain
by Amazon

32087653R00030

Ramsey had always been fascinated by the voices of the past. In parchments and scrolls, kings and warriors shouted their tales, while others whispered. However, for Ramsey, the true intrigue lay in the unsung voices, those marginalized and often rendered invisible by the very language historians used to describe them.

"Dialogues Through Time: Pronouns and the Voices of History" began as a pet project. An exploration into how pronouns shaped, and often limited, our understanding of historical narratives. How did the choice of 'he' or 'she', 'they' or 'it', shape our perception of events, of importance, of relevance?

"Dialogues Through Time: Pronouns and the Voices of History"

In the intricate tapestry of history, leaders have risen, making indelible marks that have shaped the course of events. Yet, the way we remember and narrate their stories is deeply influenced by the pronouns we use, sometimes subtly overshadowing their true essence.

In "Dialogues Through Time," Ramsey delves deep into the linguistic landscapes of history, unraveling the stories of iconic leaders from a unique vantage point. How have the pronouns used to describe Joe Biden's inclusive approach influenced our understanding of his legacy? In what ways have they echoed or contrasted with the narrative surrounding Donald Trump's polarizing tenure?

Journey back to the era of Martin Luther King, where pronouns magnified his dream and the collective aspiration of a movement. Experience Abraham Lincoln's leadership through the linguistic nuances that brought the struggles of his presidency to life. Rediscover Rosa Parks, not just as a woman who refused to give up her seat, but as an emblematic figure whose story, when viewed through the lens of pronouns, gains a deeper resonance.

Ramsey masterfully navigates the corridors of the past, challenging readers to see and hear historical narratives in a transformative light. This is not just a book about language; it's about the leaders who have defined epochs and the words that have, in turn, defined them.

Prepare to embark on a historical journey like no other—one that listens closely to the whispers between the lines and amplifies voices both familiar and forgotten.

ISBN 9798862715873

9798862715873
90000